Radio Nostalgia

CHRIS EMERY lives in Cromer with his wife and children. He works in publishing. His has written two previous collections of poetry, a writer's guide and edited editions of Emily Brontë, John Keats and Christina Rossetti. His work has been widely published in magazines and anthologised, most recently in *Identity Parade: New British and Irish Poets* (Bloodaxe, 2010). He is a contributor to *The Cambridge Companion to Creative Writing* (Cambridge University Press, 2012), edited by David Morley and Philip Neilsen.

Also by Chris Emery

POETRY
Dr. Mephisto
Radio Nostalgia
The Departure

CHAPBOOKS
The Cutting Room

WRITERS' GUIDES
*101 Ways to Make Poems Sell: The Salt Guide to Getting
and Staying Published*

AS EDITOR
Poets in View: A Visual Anthology of 50 Classic Poems
Emily Brontë: The Visionary and Other Poems
John Keats: Ode to Psyche and Other Poems
Christina Rossetti: Goblin Market and Other Poems

AS CONTRIBUTOR
The Cambridge Companion to Creative Writing,
edited by David Morley and Philip Neilsen
The Insiders' Guide to Independent Publishing,
edited by the Independent Publishers Guild
The Writer's Handbook, edited by Barry Turner

Radio Nostalgia

by

CHRIS EMERY

S
SALT

CROMER

PUBLISHED BY SALT PUBLISHING
12 Norwich Road, Cromer, Norfolk NR27 0AX, United Kingdom

First published by Arc Publications 2006
Second edition 2015

Printed and bound in the United Kingdom by Lightning Source UK Ltd

Typeset in Paperback 9 / 13

ISBN 978 1 78643 074 4 paperback

1 3 5 7 9 8 6 4 2

This book is for Jennifer

Contents

Acknowledgements

The author is grateful to the editors of the following publications, in which some of these poems, often in earlier versions, first appeared: *The Age, Cambridge Conference of Contemporary Poetry Review, Jacket, JAAM, Masthead, Parataxis, Poetry London, Poetry Review, Quid* and *Salt*.

I would like thank Kate Lithgow for providing room and space at "Crear" in Mid-Argyll, Scotland, where a number of these poems were written, conceived or dreamt of.

My grateful thanks to Angela, Tony and everyone at Arc, to John who kept me at it, and to Tony Frazer and Forrest Gander for reading the manuscript in its various disguises.

Radio Nostalgia

Tapers

Upward with tapers
death has come to meet me on the stairs.

Her face hangs like a handset on its cord
loaded with static. She always has the answers.

We are the insects of her trade
inside a world of doors.

Hereabouts she smiles and strokes
her children with aplomb,

we totter on
above the sordid rafters.

Not far off, the chimneyed landscape
rolls in black succession to the sea.

Is it that the lack of choice seems fair
within the ferment,

or that the buried coast she stalks
is feathered with ideas?

I tell her of the ghosts I've had
where each was left all tangled

in a dress shirt on the path.
We move in conical procession to the ridge.

There are stains on the knees of the officers.
Their woollen socks are grey and frayed

as we watch the minuscule dresses
soiled with distemper.

Dad, are you still in there,
shining with your tiger's eye cufflinks,

ending up in grease and pewter
in some Egyptology of the lounge?

Next I'll peer out over the cadmium earth,
jumping with the doubt of it,

my trouser hems on fire
as I race out over

sparking fibrous moorland
soaked with the milk of hinds.

Son, the oil of each memory
is a cancer for love.

Speeding with the dead can sort
whatever mouth, whatever bone.

Crear Entertainments

Out from the worn rugs
Black dogs find argument is mist
Parabolas of sheet white
Evening welter up

Heavy tears and cacophony
On the red roofs
New small boats tick below
This moment of the artefact

Elsewhere bells contend the path
Elsewhere lives whorl-up like ferns
Forked under moons
Life is all puppetry

In a second the pretty trees will swill
Or ache with fat moss
And adhere to the smallest context of it
Gothic clouds descending on

The dream harp shedding
Iron heads
In the sea
The mothers overreach to tell of it

Complaining at the kisses
Resting with sneaking folklore on
The chopped-down barley culture
Wolves and shore light

Now we find the lewd
Are truly beautiful
Berserk with marriage and marquetry
Like roasting waters below the nets

Sunday and all but the yeast night
Our lanes' determination cankered
With otters
Kneading fish beside this

Radio nostalgia
The funny dances are soft returning flakes of youth
In an incomplete sun
Every ham is scorched

While in our coats we stiffen for news
Of modern endings
Automata shelving distance
In this chat-away skin

2.

The land is a dish of brisket and roots
Some cures are fickle and stave off the band

Our old punchers are balding as freight-loads head off
For sinecures of wood and it all appears to be easy

With wire and stone in the wet mouth spinning
And we are on the dependent monstrous acre

Black loathing ploughing in angles for a plague
New lessons and judgement in tune with us

Sun tapes its leather head to the fence and gapes for
November weapons jumping at the cart

In this local ash pit were we raised robotically?
Nodding for a fixed price and a purple cut of skirt

It flourishes there within the marrow it simpers in the egg
Harbouring what tiny entrecôtes of earth

3.

Ever comes to pile
His hands on 'horse hill'

Ever comes to boil
Before this rhododendron mirror in all his facets and medals

Everyone is smiling about the wheat quota
Ecstatic with their flails

Long-attempted fields disgorge themselves
In the parish

The feeding hills
Let down their wigs

The rich fires
Belch out their narrative tantrums

For the children to take up
Rind upon rind

Like the wheels of
A tune

Black Flake

In the dream the man falls but does not drown,
Coaxed from a bed of white pine needles,
Shocked and late in winter air, falling to earth.
The man is no more than a pelt stripped from aspen
Or cherry. We see him so.

In the dream he spoils through rains
Like a black flake. A calm precise shadow
Above the lungfuls of seed and heather,
Like an idea of pressure solved in skin.
We see the days eke out their measure in white jute.

We hear the oaks in their untidy creaking,
Sifting and yearning. Years ago,
He lifted his hair in rage for the bloodless archipelago.
Now we find our mind centred on his fall,
Making this studious journey to earth.

There is no disdain. No pain or shoal of fact.
The mushrooms fold their battles in their jealous dens.
The ferns collapse into their own miasma. The man repeats
    his fall,
Pushing through branches, leaving his heart
In the dank reticulation.

In the dream, the man sheds ten thousand memories of skin.
He sees the goats and spiders crossing the deserts.
He sees the cities rising and the dirty altars ferrying rains
Up to the monsters of the populous. There is no let up
It seems. His eyes like eggs in the clinkers of his face.

[7]

The Journey

for Roddy Lumsden

When called, near our favourite moors, too soft to bear an ache this
    winter,
beyond the frozen lines of washing left out late and rigid as a mind,
I'll come and stake my life on the bare land to declare not hate
or love or municipal indifference, but kind extension. The way the traffic
purls along the road through the steep night, or that clacking of a train
pouring over Failsworth to end up here is just a black journey we could
    make
through northern narratives towards a bad nativity scene or cave of light.
Yes, here in the mill towns and dead collieries I'll hand you a note,
nothing grand or preposterous, a simple common sentence about that
    raging day
that no one could escape from, and then the barriers will fall, Roddy, to
    show
receding light up there on that hill monument, like some invite to
    another life.

The Candidates

I am the shadow of the moth
Old moth with nice tails and a loose eye

Watching black reruns
In smoky vanilla and tulle motel rooms

I have fifty clear objectives today
And a presbyterian necklace

No coward will placate
In the afternoon

I am instilled
With fabric and purpose

Here is the low concrete and metal gearing
Of the breeding ramps the ramps

The rich could race forward from away from the Left
Pure and free of idiolectic glamour

No teeth or handles on the solid body anymore
Alone again in the lymph reactor

Everything displaces the natural power of things
Calm and oblivious the heroes are

Hissing in the turbine room
With that old medicine of boots (too many boots)

And then this interrupted retching
On the mighty cinnamon rubbish of the earth

Endless Banks

1.

tall mouth in bronze vestiges
a mouth stationed in 30°
shadowless pole or rotating bite line

feeder road and patched
asphalt six or seven stains outside
inside coffee with barren rag

and plasticised arterial
vending with other columnar
lighting in vernal orange clusters

2.

prehensile stumps above
white batter of polystyrene grid
cubic rotational staff plan

wood with crumb-filled
pocket menu sunny haven
angled with star-flashed salad bar

heightened magenta
and cyan irregular empty
pan booth just beside it

3.

cartoon gold chest
signal surge and filter where
pine redolent verge opens

on to stave-marked esplanades
with shabby cap
(expanded Foamex™ or Foamcore™ bins)

and black neutrinos or
escalation of loaded glare free from
hydrogenated meat complex

4.

measured tolerant net to
seating system with heady build
rated ten for loading cleft

with $47°$ angle and scapular ease
unrestrained circulating
aircon convex killer skirt

the flow back shows thirty-four
mouths stooping and biting
on the residue

Loose Meat

In my freak-show days
On the *cusp of empire*
Soapy hands on twenty ideal sacs
Weaseling for the sound committee

I'd come on all night as ribs
And chalk in the northern trips
Marking time before each signal petered out
By bobbing turds and the chiselled

Life of the escarpment
Making every eye ache at the Prefecture
All kettles and crumbs
Lapping up capacity for ruinous days

There then / as if a fillet in
Perpetual amber articulated solder wings
Grunted for local cabbage
For improvised pork (all pins and mustard)

I'm staking teeth on it
Here at broadcast depth
Shaving off each dirty hole as I rinse
And rinse the steakhouse knives

Old gasoline farts and echoes as I say
Beyond the soiled retinal glare
My town's ratings fused with lead
Still pleasuring the wreck of Mother

One can sit and burn intrusive meat
Recording the one chair in a violet room
Each long stew of tongues
Toiling the pan in the blunt lounge

It is (as promised) all here for you now
Wrapped in dog skins / wrapped in lungs
The contraband of little men
Gasping in a bed

Sewer Music for the Social Bargain

I want to punish Tony's mouth
And reach across his chest

Outside the pitch and gloss of fresh water
Outside the jangling

Leisure crews
Re-establish the holy life of the cure

Watching with cupped hands I see the petrol century
The terminus empty

As though wrapping tiny feet in hearts and crowns
And spying the broken flag of your head

Would soothe each seg flannel and tart
In some attempt at ruin or skid and skid

To the uplift of the combined assassination frame
No more then than a dub band

Or plastic idle monster
Nightly flaming on her skin

Your furious resolve
Is sin

And through it all we dream of buttons
Shaped like kids' ears and toes

Okay the arse of the earth can supply
Its pipes and whirlpools

Tonight though we can stray together
Inside the mongrel life of truth

Shining with such seminal tunes of detox borax
Nude swill

We laugh about all day
Or like this fade within the treasure box

Let's kill this mealy city
We are royal insects and fabulous lux

Tan-coloured perfect once and for all
Imagine the life beneath your kiss

The liars rushing to breaking Fox glamour
The plebeian anchor sinking her retake

Showing habitual glass sides
And the buses of the candidate

Caught in beards of smoke
Returning such metal answers and some form of

Cauterised imperial factories
Smoking

Too sallow
For wintry armour

And the electrification of the soul
Those high causal notes above magnificent forests

Sufficient for the grave and yes
This is so beautiful now

A life fit for burning expostulation
Moistened with the fuel of the ghost

From the Centre

Once your eyes have adjusted to the grit
and sprawl of Braille around the tableaux
you'll see ears are ammonites, hands starfish,
and tilt your head to watch the weather's slow

procession from the dig. There's singing or crying
investing wealth with high-throated commotion.
At midday the daylight ends; no one wings it
in the compound. We are poverty in motion.

How we ended up here is funny, like a shiny
belly or bare flank, or it could be that ash-
coloured, hose-damp concrete there.
Every child distorts the man and man the cash.

Look at it raining down — atrocious love
beside couples filming or are they fleeing
the gift. It is an entirely live feed as we learn dogma
from wire. Someone says, 'Nomads in waiting,'

and we become scintillating, free in the debris.
Don't catch life out, then, and watch the traffic.
Now you know, when the slap up meals fall out
of those sacks, we'll be taking home our pick

of your bomb-retiring heroes, day and night,
night and day, those clean-cut silent flags of ham-
burger heaven still warm under props. Later, we'll
be zooming or seething through that dream

of dislocated empty routes, shaky gorgons
of the zone. Together we are a modern fog,
the idea of the better dead, immortalised grey
eyes above subtitled totally idealised dialogue.

No one adheres to the precise terms any more.
The streets shiver like widows this afternoon of very
large government. We'll ape out the speeches
of the ape. This country is his artery.

Dog Face

O climbing dog face
Beleaguered story of the beard

Lost in this columbarium
And light-spoiling surgery

Watching limbs
At spastic points along

The boulevard
With eglantine and zinc

The eggy brickwork
And tamping tamping

Hell of hands
Or praised surfactants

Everything is soot-black need
Igniting waving flags

Muntjack and ideologues
The swollen tongue

The swollen
Heart

And jupiter rising
Like a wart

Over magisterial glass
And peculiar mental bruising

Skinny still
The boiling oaks

That studied nodal haulage
Smoking or

Falling like superior quilt on
White corporate acres

And resistances of piccolos
Still sweet at that

December

Distraught on the Vlatava
Drilled in moist
Government an
Almost inseparable
Loyalist infirm
Fibre
Un-

Played
Before sections
Bending to the task
Beds played out
Foremost
Glazes pronounced

Tre-
Pan
Trepan-
Ning
Gild-
Ed
Choronzon
Fielding the same
Said thing in stems or
Bays about the head
Ablaze

For cordite and meals
Simply echoes
For virtuous

Inviolable
Clods

Bone cost
Featured in sealed
Elijah trucks
Keeping time
Through island sounds

Ig-
Nited arms
Waving in flaps
From the singing
Paraphernalia
Of dead
Nights

Cold Twig Men of the Future

Shaking hand
Its stitches fill
Cold twig men
In Kelso town

Stone purchase
All we own of Spring
Still arguing
Discordantly

Ah signal shapes
Stretched
Root hair our
Final mouths

And moon-eyed
Girls the sheep
And stars twisting
Eating beets through

New days of tun
Logic placing
Field choirs in
Odourless scar

Over the military den
Love is calcium
Head song too
And trim flannels

In the fiery citadel
Burning amber
Or rust-verdigris
Our aeon aches

The farms return
Their chalk lines
The crops their
Insect heart

Saturniidae

liver child I smell your
teats above cold drapes
and the cordons of the

tender shrimp
sends its rancid powers
through the dream

the tower shrieks
is perched on
its finely chopped walls

of earth
rising from that lung
the perfect surveillance of

hills of willow herb
and cow parsley
of dirty troves

your twisting face
is goat breath
and the hope of mass

why does skin
go singing through
each night in flames

I fasten on the tidal
towns of Emperor moths
their oriflamme

gap of object fervour
brightest thigh
of art

and moons where
we are turned so low
so pistillate

so distillate
in trailing sink
with lovely paper forms

Pornographic Leg Song

In umber rain
The leg stomped on

Grey rapture of coal towns
Lanes of dead cypresses

With Silver Ds of sheriff's feet
On the hardly-worn chiffon

In the canalised scrub
The soft arterial motor

Where silver forests hold
What battalions of the heart

Grow weaker by eye-light
The infants infect muscle

Under gold-embroidered
Mesopotamian nights

Their berets flying
Towards the brassy sun

It fell (the leg)
A little happy thing

Lying there cramped-up
With a feral look

The wardens came
With mop & bucket

Bringing Windowlene
To polish & pamper

The limb
Trustees rigged a dais

To mask the features
Of the idealistic crop

& spot the liver-coloured
Ravages they warmed too

By the samovar & wet-sheet
There is vintage condensation

On fuzzy glass where the limb
Enjoys its indolent kisses

Faces fêting and prayers and votes
And the intercession of the dream

Bone Merchant

No peace then, more then, worse,
An apostasy of limbs
For sorting kinds of architecture,
Pipes and troughs, the rouge countenance
Gone in the mouth as we washed
Her lavish steaks staining fingers
In the pepper earth. Particular
Lies on apostolic flames failing the soft
Cathedrals and sensing still the
Bone merchant. We can take them
In mad creels. Slowly then low cloud
On shaking plains melted off the pelts
And the trees and blackthorn.
The crow-matched formula inventing
Height like a bomb. Our unwieldy outgrowth
Coalesced in moth flight.
More resonance pasted to twin legs.
Then we see the engine on its
Armature and feral cause,
Rickety, with no culmination
In prepared things, no heart then,
Passing back its tiny glove fictions,
Its arc of hats and columbines.
Are we saturated? Massively
Redundant? The gum anthems
Riskily packaged in a wadge
Of suits, all meagre and infirm in the
Queues, ears poking from gelding nests
And this short sort of butchery. Stitchery
Fine, but so provincial. The doctors

Spinning in their world dance
For lassitude and fresh country.
The candidates laid bare, counting
Their hands ringed with iron as the pump
Mended our throats, primed and lifted
30,000 gallons or more to knock
The youth, cherishing each pattern
In the rock and lifting the glassy
Stirrups. The humans all leaving then
To free the mouth of hope. As if
The stars could not unleash our end.
And no supersession of the heart.

Clan Tinnitus

Burn the bishops and those of our children sour and blind
And the Oracle DBAs burn them
Burn the police and those who crack the spines of the rosters

And anyone maintaining the vertiginous self-compiling records
Of the lazy and weak and those who demand respect or loyalty
Burn them and all the literary officers in Sheffield and Droylsden

Then burn the barristers
Especially them for their A-line dresses and tort
And the soldiers and teachers burn them serving the servants

And the phlebotomists in their handsome corridors
And bankers golfers huntsmen
And those academics not reflexive enough

And of course
The whispering rags
Of the Left

Burn them stab them in the throat and eyes
Let them crawl with holes in them paraffin and excrement
Burn them for love for hope burn them

Destroy the open fields and smile over the peeling segmentation of it
As though the merciful were true let them burn
For they are social monsters

And we ought to intend
For some clarity of purpose
When arranging the derelict year

And in the remnants of a town and its post-industrial canal
And in your neighbourhood with its weak survey of negligence
Idle brick-bottomed streets and all the knives and needles

Pile them pile them great heaps of them and burn them
And burn and burn and burn them
Keep on burning and burning until

Only the scholastic pleasure of dullards and wasters
Can feel the throat of justice arching for breath
Or the life of art sinks into their palms and can you hear the trauma
         of it

Until you can feel their eyes opening on the blood dawn of it
The white lawns and crisp vestiges of the estates
Let them walk among the ash pits of the estates

Stalking the orderly insistence of it
The practical inclination of it the good of the poor
For this is our nation and we are free

The Impresario

I've been asked to choke up
The listeners

With some words and grunts from
The 36 chambers

Throwing down sound like
A road

Except I am torn now
And broken

With the rifling god to be saved
Along with my controller

In the augmentation
Of the zoo bomb

All the endings are cages
In time

In this theocracy
Of factory cysts

Like an idea
Swaying under wings of lead

Muchachos imagos immortelles
Mouthing total ruin

Over shining trays of teeth
No afterlife

Deep enough to censure
The shrink-wrapped dolls

I know we can entrust this
To image creep

And pre-judicial hearings
Where the ostentatious skulls

Of feral law
Are turned to Braille

Our sons debauch
The glamourous slums

With prayer conventions
Stalking dojos at Showtime

On a comedown
With every must-have nude

Beyond the convex personae
Of the Mayor

Or that Martian ray gun summer tilt
At the Holy Mother

Uprooting pathetic dance steps
While every angle

Joins the Institute of Wounds
My cowboy sling back

Zulu militia
Washing fallow bones

In the countdown to armaments
On Zorba Street

Henry Purcell's Love Song

Oval night and oval day
Our smiling governor rests
And crocodiles guest

In farting ascension
With dancing sailors
In their sails up high

Or in the ruptured fields of silt
Please hear us naked Dido
In bitter gusts

And Nile song
Have fear
Have fear

From the frozen local chamber
Burnt umber piping
Stripped on stiff ground

This maximal stare
And anal toy
Will love the giddy days

Our towers fixed
And treacle saints
In facing history

Note each simple cycle
Flowing with
Cinnamon or kerosene

And barking purple cells
Show gold night gold
Day and tell us

Of purpose sunk in coral skin
And praise of new ideas
And wide electric surf

Where viols are drunk on porter
The draftsman ill
His flourish shows the mitres

And our monstrous head
Of ridding fleas and grease
Love's borders increase

The Mouths of Sweet Virginia

Feed upon mouths
Meadowsweet and nacre
The burning field
And crux of lupins

Opening beside
The smashed taupe
Wheat & brick
No sound alone

Or apostasy
In grey fog
Head in the pan
The sweat-gang

Steadily purchasing
Its love cast
Radium
Head shot

Jaw-line gone
And dirty features
In grey drives
The narrative

Translucent
Among sublimely
Tight machines
You hear our blue calls

Among silage
Attending
To the crisper tales
Of ballooning might

Grenadine & puce
With foetal warmth
And something or other
Cooing down the lanes

Moving the ciphers
Separately hardened
In *that* firmament
Of white blood

My Heraldic Ape

Special curvature of
The ape not ape
But degradation
Of the bud

Smiling flapping heap which the
Daybreak clutter *sisters*
Affectionate
beside

Our wan distortion booth
And forwards to the news
In scales and flags
The partial helmet filled

With showy heavy
Ambergris
Or anthracite below
The glamourous

Stirrups of the throat
Watching us watching
The rickety decks
Of a habitus

Solving not solving
But suffering the
Future with us
Just the same

No weekly chemistry
Creaking within
The soft consolations
Of an attack

The Spiders of the Just

We are entering the studio
Smiling & holding our chitties
The host pours TV pots
On trays of tiny spiders

As we wash each utensil
Licking the songs of the future
In this elemental sink
Over there the *wrecks* are stuck

In the family of petrol waters
But here we are kissing
The factory trough
Making some suggestion

About these lungs & arrogant
Fittings / the bolts
On the hearts of our kids
The vacuum of youth

Or some tidy truth
& so with our bones
Shrieking with crows and poised
Lascivious on the right path

We love our host / his phosphorus
Mouth all talk again
On the majesty of this gas
& worried we still sing

Squatting on happy faces
Staring straight through
To the fingers working
In the fat beautician's clinic

Or else it is us ruining
Some old pneumatic country
Awkward birds still loose
Beyond this evening's wires

Listen we got this for you
Free from crutches
Yanking on the shade
Of years to come

Strain all dog thought
To fathom out these feet
(We saw them once in the *fridge*)
& putting necessary love in mind

Just yesterday you ruined ten
But now their solid dresses flutter
As we play tig in the yard
Beside the old distillery drum

Yes here it is before you go
Into the tirade of wild motors
With your thoughts snacking
On cold stone

Grand Ole Arm Opry

Gamelan music
Puffs along the veldt and so
Amid amber stalks

Modified for trust
And up the scarp beside
Gold swingeing angels

That seem to kill the lark
We have hymns
On carmine soil

The beautiful dancing
Of severed arms with
Lilac clouds rooting and

Lobbing hermeneutics
The fuchsias fizz and snag
But the arms are tasty still

Here among the sows
Our mind is one yet so
Priapic in its purpose

Of uplift and resurgence
I still love the realists
And correct their modulus

The stomach gone
The roughened edges
No use for counting impact

Penetration it seems
The arm (in shades of cadmium)
Like Spinoza runs in dirt

The arm in space as Svabo has it
Opens the spectating worm
Among thorny rickets

Wild-haired councillors piss
In bourgeois arpeggios
And lead us to this kiss

The clutching stems
Of backward-noise of
Empty arias

Distance & black earth
As the gannet barks
And overhead the cradles spill their coal

Onto some wire rut
Of sea
That perfect recipe

Class Narratives for Art

Outside the shop of our
Arc-lit Tin-Tin singalong
Is moon-yellow youth

We are not quite
Putative going up the rungs
With fussy suits

Prismatic
Glazing
Cities

Just like this now
Besotted
With avenues of tar

The offices spotted
With semen & tar
I can take it all to mean

Some solid impact
On the trade release figures
Or a ghost

Of the idea of wolves
Sadly ardent
In petrol frost

2.

Kindled perhaps
With dogs
Inside her

Mountains of mites
& thin ice
Above the coffin

Knitted out in skin
& daytime reckoning tv
A mike & red meat

& the concomitant
Whining
Like the Christian idea

Of a window
On the soul
Smashed & leprous

& then I said
That all around
Are hairs

She was my bristling flâneur
Taken at once
Pincered urban & savvy

3.

She was my
Territory & smiting place
In the absolute tear of now

Teetering or cavalier
Held there to steer a space
Between gravity

To occupy this tiny
Space this
Bald heart

With an eye for
Shelving
& the animals upon it

So much lace
& desiderata
Bleeding endlessly

Through this shoal
Today I shall dance
My tiger dance

& conjure her
A life tarter than my own
Brutal & young as this nib

4.

As a support
For the cold basin of the soul
This bed

Or bone yard
As always
Takes good stock

(she said)
Of bindings
And fleshy schemata

But they must be tight
Tight as the clasps
Of the soul

We need it that tight
As our ribs will know
Partially at least

The killer's unremitting
Tongue
Like a bandage

Staunching a wound
And the climax written
In every eye

Broadcasts

Take the smell of those creatures
Parading in fuel or lying
In gold mud beside the yew trees
From which in shame-shards
Sound's incandescent worms rang out
We loved it / bright bones lapping
Up the soiled water charging
For an hour above the regional blaze
Each one asking for the gilded queue
Tired from the staves of wires
Or spurning the approved argot
To burn troops and kiss each glove
Listening then or barging in
Among leather fanfares foisting off
A thousand tonnes of limbs
Each night aborts its remedy
Tense and tidy as a carcass
With rented cars flourishing
Where we sat pent-up like muscles
The guidelines preferred betrayal
Quavering in the dance cabinet
Lumped-in as tapes spewed on
About the buoyant feasting
Was it grace stripping Mother
Fingering the total wreck?
We blamed the shadows in unison
Pale arms above the mono crop
Go go my shitty metal future
Sweating on drifting skirts
As pale ducts flare with teeth

The sick brigades empty out
The fan stinks beside the children
Wheels spinning where bearings
Continuously squeal vis-à-vis
Offal and headscarves a razor
Or needle scraping the valves of
Slow fucking divertimentos
Whose blue ears destroyed the cell
As each foetal lung broadcasts
Over white eiderdowns
Over the brightest informants
With tiny faces shaved off
Upholding the smoking Secretariat
The screaming gates still
Miles beyond each perfect meal

Gingham Debt Relief

how this snow face
this orange road
succeeds beyond oak

where neighbours sing of apes
or the copper names
then check the walls

all we have lent them
is musculature
the coast is interstitial now

where we crave
severe isolate remnants
hips and feet and violet hills

where the stars turn and ears
climb the paddocks
tubercular with the second tips

of the carcass
naked with
the mouth of

the sheep the black
lanes where our children lost
complete surveillance
exhausts thought
and wearily
frames the spit of land

the clouds as we smile are colder now
piling their sagas
in sacral balloons

bankers of the earth
more tired than art
are thankfully killing off nations

and we keep the tidy pitch
for our brothers
in the borders

the spinster in the ditch
nostalgia takes her candles
through the limescale pools

and staggers breathless
drowning not drowning reaching
with those silken arms

wasps settled on the stone lung
managing
the levy

The Curtain

It's no good maintaining appearances. I am not
as I was. I'm keeping out of things. Still muttering
and picking my skin. Just noise in the rubble. The
curtains shifting, a little musty, as the engineers
prepare the way. Out there the seats are all empty.
Where have I got to in the course of events? It is of
no consequence. The words teeter and genuflect,
little obelisks moist in the dusk. There are limbs of
course, but none of them are mine. Someone else
is at work on things. For a long time I have been
participating in my own eradication. There is no
end to this. The blade scrapes and scrapes. The
bleach makes its mark. A fossil burns in the grate.
I sense I can make things clean again. The scene
is almost clean. Cleanliness is very important.
A machine scrabbling in the dust, picking its
templates, picking its phrases. A machine burning
for delivery. Cleanliness is unquestionably a very
important part of making a contribution. Building
the erratic gorgeous system. It is extremely pure
and deprived of all identity. For a long time I have
known that things are perfect. I have decided to
get to the heart of this issue. As I make progress
I am not clear I am in the midst of beauty. This is
very liberating and also sour, like the taste of zinc.
Sometimes I imagine I can matter, but largely this
is a fabrication and completely disgusting. Once I
have become another my life will be worth living.
Until then the scrubbing seems a lustful and
egocentric waste of time. Only after I have gone will

the system become clear. I cannot get to the dark bed. The frontier is very cold and uncomfortable. Soon it will have to end.

Municipal Care Foundation

love the governed edges too
its curlicues and torcs
its windows with their wispy nylon features

yes the Municipal Care Foundation
is my shattered loafing future
this abdomen dug up so that the

limpid index curving
not thriving on the static pile
of buoyant metal

sagged at the pumiced tip
where the eye slits
governed the body's crazy pagodas

2.

inch and torpor
the straw brain of the wind
on haunch-red distance

infants torch
or boast of
the lead community

naked reflex & *amour*
with swirling ruddy soldiers
falling in an arc

of tight perfume
their faecal souterrain & armatures
outstretched for a kiss

3.

severe polished tin
the new canvas over bodies
sews a stunning sea beyond the fat corona

we are one single mass
poised with clamps and engines
roaring continual order

with the failure of ideas
bending and straightening each
white soul

masks and thumbs
gentle shoulders not leavening
the zipped-up sack

George's Song

While we must stare
And love disease
In leisured sunny days
The final crow ejecting
And you my mind again
All through the knocks
A cheap sand snatching
That seas cannot time
The quartz palaver

Stating this and thick in worn
Pyjamas again a loss of
Breathing then hawking
To itch on pale distemper
The silver flanks
Of fat and felt
In mild grey tonnes
By wild doors calls a town
A sudden extravagance
That strays well from
Cold localised herds
Justice reeks at sky's bevel
Stones fattened on pillows
Stones fattened on milt
A monstrance tipped again
Otherwise else in shingles
Keeps you out keeps you
In worn adulation
Ticking for the bowel crime
Rockaby queer free one now

Rockaby rockaby

The microphone
Is dead as postures now
Engines purl on purple
Indiscriminate anvils
Touching the wavehead
Headphones cracking
Whilst mother at her wash
Mouth tense ash face
Frozen up in mud wet
Seething over yellow
Caul taut and packed
With violet scenes
Of change how dear how dear
Our corporate dances
Lifting bony boxes
And soiled cubic rage
To freshen this pancreatic
Parliament

All first to time's
Sour luggage
Our shadow kept for extra
As each feathery
Proboscis scrapes across
Our tiny scales
Music failed in little days
On shifting

[63]

Entelechy a mass in which
Imperfect azimuths are love
Your sloping girl blue
Haunches glissade on stains
Over tolerant cable
The wire clear the den bright
As mouth tense ash face
Frozen up in mud wet
Knees bent to ideas
Bent as old grass still
Toils a weakened pelt
Outside the good room

Now nickel draft of tears
Iron sheets and troops
Happy under tensile steel
Happy under total
Blasting the info good
Condensing in what core
Fandango
Face still hung
The cables wet above
Ten thousand
Eyes still sagging ailing
Beyond the positronic
Cleats of will
As shoddy lips
Enunciate the bitter searches
Yet again all again
A tonic for what void as

[64]

Sharpest teeth go chatter
Chatter blighting now
And biting
On the measled grapes
The tongue in its waxy haven
Shoving on and on
Cheering frozen gulls
While lips invoke
A money shot stuttered
With the tousled stars
Replete by that perspex
Room amplified but mute
Mouthing still
And still unsaid
While we can stare

And spell our pale disease
In leisured sunny days

The Lermontov

The cruise ship was
A weak heart grinding.
Weighing in cold presence
The grief.

The Lermontov fathoming
Industrial pine beside the tiered
Ice cliffs. In its wake
That month of bells

Our crew embraced Lenin.
He boiled on lapels,
His savage index and globe
Ardent, dilapidated thesis,

Yet no red life was made.
Ideas foiled the smashing
Waves and boiled under
The manoeuvre's wasting feature.

New negative horizons
Fused the common purpose.
The natal sea was antic. The lanes showed
Severe ash drop permanence

Making life its excavation.
Ancestors in leather
Jewelled fields and outcrops
Were just tattoos of earth.

Years sunk in black throats.
The ruined heads of bears stared
From the intaglio of it.
3,000 miles below

The frozen heart
Still spins with abstraction.
We adhere to its iron crystal,
Faster, darker polyps,

Love's scouring creatures,
Electric weight unbedding
The banal arc
Of the salt path.

Yellow Shattered Waters

1.

Chicken-frieze Motown wreck
where insects crack their music
in the mall

my son tans his waist
beside some hills of wire
and sagging concrete plateaux

form a complete roost
with low res screeds of gilding
on wet joists

which forms one ideal backdrop
to this inland sea
of contraflows

2.

Down the years
ten thousand feet
of smiles

form the thin white lips of the shore
and Tulsa raptures
devoting crab juice

no more then
than calm shells
beside her corn blue eyes

and his decision to leave
to make an occasion
for the long-expected prick fanatic

3.

Resting in the packing plant
underneath cool
peptide skies

& wan Cartesian
episodes in
cocaine

we all retrieve
a muscle
O warm milk

of the Urals
bending under jugs of flames
beside the jug man

4.

In whom a syllable
languishes
and alters these waters & their

solo banquet of boots
in Matzo meal
& clearance methods

chiding rusting boats
escaping the orange earth
the lifeless donor

in out of radio echoes
choosing each leaf
with echoes of gold

5.

In the white forest
shaving shaving loyal shaving
forest of the head

bulbous feeder pack
stitching the panic of rocks
& crumbling gold

& then the levitation
again above each vexed
somatic herd

on champagne concrete
plateaux dripping on
the turkey shoot of city suitors

The Wolves are on the Dark Beef

the wolves are on the dark beef
surrounding the cannery

Tony lift your hand
and share this blanket now your burning feet

can go ahead and walk the border
aching winter racing order

fidgeting with your neighbour's plaits
with neutral meat the steady state

one measure is a form of rent
another the escarpment

but calmer now we count the beads
and touch the cysts of Islam

2.

she has wept for the creatures for years
within that featured arbour *just look at it*

set below these sticks
and skinned gods

until majesty seeps from each menagerie
to charge the soul

old shoals and interim dark
the stained folks keep waiting

so fine beyond the cinematic hunt and blur
levitating from their holes

carnal yes
but maculate

3.

feasting here the royal tides are only green
like minutes in the throat

the planets drop and I can see their ruined hulks increase
capable and raging we nearly rectify the tower

the golden viscous breath has new artillery too
time's smear woven in the river grass

no intermediate vein or cure within this incursion
or cull of selves and then the street is sick with sand

wishing us far from neutered arms
a loss planed from some colossal wood

with tooting sign and tooting skin no sign no sin
in the benzene motorhome

4.

that vascular slit of rubber articulates our pastel night
monitored by cameras in juts of life

there is delight in feathers you can imagine
the sofa party forked cradle old future and cyborg

kiss the blasting episode again
who cares for this idea cramped in some rigger's panic

and the wild body draped
we drink for the wasp days so few now

below the
white paste of years

it is all so loose
inside the feeding plant

Blemish

Let me in your dirty mouth
To cram black flakes queer doll
In the rubric of your breath
Or tarnished meat tracks
Beneath the desiccated fields
Of porcelain and tench

Have me swing through hips
Along coal avenues and jaws
To pierce the joists
Far from this dump
As electric mobile children
Force upon pips

My gorgeous oligarchy
Let it still pump through
The Institute to choose hair
Endlessly over gravure lungs
As we race above farm air
To spill each shot

So let your filthy mouth
Exercise the triumvirate
Or engineer fur sockets
In love of torn cloth
On the pressurised tanks
With this investiture of eyes

To move each out among
The reels and teeth
And leech our proper channels
While the leather futures end
In tides and chrome winds
At last

Then hear the wittering readers
Charm each hit from
Fleets in rusting mud drifts
Beside the Spartan halls
Among healing processions
And planks of food again

While frequencies continually
Yield their singeing eyelids
As the dead seeds burst
By each fat captain
Under a gorgeous chemical
Monologue

Lemnos Revisited

after Sophocles

Along the road beyond a sign or mention of it
I came to in the dead light of Lemnos
I hear their war cries and will not heal

So they left me stinking among the rocks
To ponder the rich shade of Chrysa's shore
And think of the Achaean feasts

Abandoned on the land without succour
And only abstract rags and this reconnaissance
My heart has no pity

Watching the dark tiers of the earth steer
Like some neutral star path in the sea
While yet across the sea I hear Paris

Shouting a new method of glory
Consider us dragging that shining horse of flame
Seething in the dark resin

We were always spiralling to Troy
Sinking with the earth's turning fury of love
Affection and attack

Now far away these chafing women
Are my border watch and know the facts of it
Shaking a lifetime of winding sheets

I hear the war drum and the scissors of men
So let this ink pool of the gods explain
Our designified wounds

Our lack of monuments in this final order
My military effort can host no creed
No glaze or feature except the posture

And rancour we hold to be just
For in this local output deficit we may trade
The chaos of our meals for a white cage

I know no thought will mar that furious life
My ranging shot and perfect cut
Will spur the vaulted hills

Straight to the feathery heaps discarded there
I will see our little treasures wasted
The earth bandaged up

I'll hear their fricatives and see their plastic torsos
Hot above our hot post-animate shells
Pastel vexed and torpid

Pressed in the teeth of the wheels
The steel pigs mashing down
With terminal velocity

www.ingramcontent.com/pod-product-compliance
Lightning Source LLC
Chambersburg PA
CBHW022036090426
42741CB00007B/1092